The

QUOTABLE

The
QUOTABLE

Walt Disney

Compiled by
Dave Smith

EDITIONS

Los Angeles • New York

ISBN 0-7868-5332-8

For information address
Disney Editions
1101 Flower Street
Glendale, California 91201

Design by Polly Kanevsky

Library of Congress Catalog Card Number: 00-60128

Printed in the United States of America

First Edition

10 9
FAC-020093-16062
ACKNOWLEDGMENTS:

The Quotable Walt Disney was compiled by Dave Smith, director of the Walt Disney Archives. Dave is the author of *Disney A to Z* and the coauthor of *The Ultimate Disney Trivia Books* 1 through 4 and *Disney: The First 100 Years.*

Thank you to Randy Bright, Rebecca Cline, Jennifer Hendrickson, Rose Motzko, Bob Schneider, Paula Sigman, Ed Squair, and Robert Tieman.

Visit www.disneyeditions.com

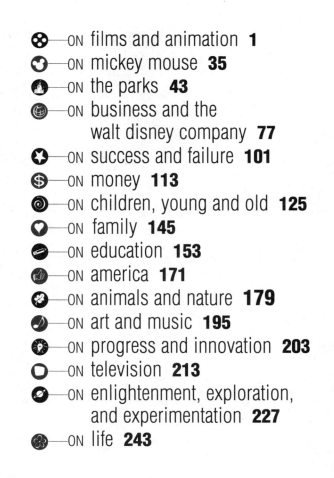
contents

on films and animation

"Because the eye is the most sensitive and dependable of our sense organs, the motion picture offers the widest, direct avenue to our emotions. Whereas the still picture can suggest only a fragment of fact or fiction, the cartoon-in-motion is without limit in communicating ideas, events, and human relations."

"The motion picture has become a necessity of life, a part of our balanced existence. It is not a negligible luxury. People are always going to demand and enjoy movies in the theater. Perhaps not as exclusively as they did when public amusements were more limited. Patronage will depend more than ever upon what we put on the screen. And especially on how well we understand the needs and desires of our younger customers. For their favor we must compete as never before."

"The business has grown continuously through these years, although at times the road was rocky. But I don't know of any other entertainment medium that can give to the millions of families the world over more value than the motion picture."

"Nothing in a lifetime of picture making has been more exciting and personally satisfactory than delving into the wonders, the mysteries, the magnificent commonplaces of life around us and passing them on via the screen."

"'Well, in order to crack the field,' I said, 'I've got to get something a little unique, you see.' Now, they had the clown out of the inkwell who played with the live people. So [with the *Alice Comedies*] I reversed it. I took the live person and put him into the cartoon field. I said, 'That's a new twist.' And it sold. I was surprised myself."

"People still think of me as a cartoonist, but the only thing I lift a pen or pencil for these days is to sign a contract, a check, or an autograph."

"To captivate our varied and worldwide audience of all ages, the nature and treatment of the fairy tale, the legend, the myth have to be elementary, simple. Good and evil, the antagonists of all great drama in some guise, must be believably personalized. The moral ideals common to all humanity must be upheld. The victories must not be too easy. Strife to test valor is still and always will be the basic ingredient of the animated tale, as of all screen entertainments."

"Speaking for the one field which I feel definitely qualified to comment on, I fully believe the animated picture will emerge as one of the greatest mediums, not only of entertainment but also of education."

"Cartoon animation offers a medium of storytelling and visual entertainment, which can bring pleasure and information to people of all ages everywhere in the world."

"I started, actually, to make my first animated cartoon in 1920. Of course, they were very crude things then and I used sort of little puppet things."

"To translate the world's great fairy tales, thrilling legends, stirring folk tales into visual theatrical presentations and to get back warm response of audiences in many lands have been for me an experience and a lifetime satisfaction beyond all value."

"In learning the art of storytelling by animation, I have discovered that language has an anatomy. Every spoken word, whether uttered by a living person or by a cartoon character, has its facial grimace, emphasizing the meaning."

"Animation is different from other [live-action] film. Its language is the language of caricature. Our most difficult job was to develop the cartoon's unnatural but seemingly natural anatomy for humans and animals."

"Animation can explain whatever the mind of man can conceive. This facility makes it the most versatile and explicit means of communication yet devised for quick mass appreciation."

"I take great pride in the artistic development of cartoons. Our characters are made to go through emotions which a few short years ago would have seemed impossible to secure with a cartoon character. Some of the action produced in the finished cartoon of today is more graceful than anything possible for a human to do."

"To think six years ahead—even two or three—in this business of making animated cartoon features, it takes calculated risk and much more than blind faith in the future of theatrical motion pictures. I see motion pictures as a family-founded institution closely related to the life and labor of millions of people. Entertainment such as our business provides has become a necessity, not a luxury. Curiously, it offers us the greatest reassurance about the future in the animation field. Fantasy, when properly done in the one medium best adapted to its nature, need never go stale for the family taste."

"We are not trying to entertain the critics. I'll take my chances with the public."

"Moviemakers are often too introverted about their production. They tend to build up myths about audiences and to prattle glibly about shifting public taste and its unpredictables. In considering audiences and our professional function, remember one thing: Americans are a sociable folk; we like to enjoy ourselves in crowds, at sports arenas, at picnics, fairs, and carnivals, at concerts, and at the theater. Above all, we like to laugh together—even at our own shortcomings. I don't like to kid myself about the intelligence and taste of audiences. They are made up of my neighbors, people I know and meet every day. Folks I trade with, go to church with, vote with, compete in business with, help build and preserve a nation with."

"Public taste in amusement has changed very decidedly since the early days when the motion picture was a toy, a novelty; it has changed as much in animation as in live-action cinema offerings."

"Before sitting down to count my blessings, I want to make you a promise. I promise we won't let this great honor you have paid us tonight go to our heads—we have too many projects for the future to take time out for such a thing. On top of that, after forty-some-odd years of ups and downs in this crazy business of ours, we know too well—you are only as good as your next picture."
(Taken from an awards speech)

"Films stimulate children to read books on many subjects."

"We have created characters and animated them in the dimension of depth, revealing through them to our perturbed world that the things we have in common far outnumber and outweigh those that divide us."

"Until a character becomes a personality it cannot be believed. Without personality, the character may do funny or interesting things, but unless people are able to identify themselves with the character, its actions will seem unreal. And without personality, a story cannot ring true to the audience."

"Our field of entertainment still has many new and exciting and wonderful things to bring to the restless public wanting variety and novelty in the movie theater. The only thing we should fear and be on constant guard against is getting bogged down—getting into the ruts of monotony and timeworn repetitions which the business of entertainment cannot long stand."

"All cartoon characters and fables must be exaggeration, caricatures. It is the very nature of fantasy and fable."

"I try to build a full personality for each of our cartoon characters—to make them personalities."

"In these extraordinary days we realize fully that the public is shopping more than ever for its box office fare. There is no compromise for 'selling' your attractions. I am confident that the future will enable us to fill this bill."

"More than any other medium, the motion picture is being challenged to meet the greatly enlarged opportunities and responsibilities of modern showmanship."

"Through historical time—and even among our aboriginal forefathers—all the races of man have been dramatizing these eternal quests and conquests of mind and heart; in arenas, around tribal fires, in temples and theaters. The modes of entertainment have changed through the centuries; the content of public shows, very little."

"From years of experience I have learned what could legitimately be added to increase the thrills and delights of a fairy tale without violating the moral and meaning of the original. Audiences have confirmed this unmistakably. We define the heroines and heroes more vividly; add minor characters to help carry the story line; virtually create such immortal friends of the heroine as the Seven Dwarfs. Storywise, we sharpen the decisive triumph of good over evil with our valiant knights—the issues which represent our moral ideals. We do it in a romantic fashion, easily comprehended by children. In this respect, moving pictures are more potent than volumes of familiar words in books."

"Literary versions of old fairy tales are usually thin and briefly told. They must be expanded and embellished to meet the requirements of theater playing time, and the common enjoyment of all members of movie-going families. The screen version must perceive and emphasize the basic moral intent and the values upon which every great persistent fairy tale is found. To these ends I have devoted my own best efforts and the talents of my organization, in full realization of our responsibility as a mass entertainer and especially our responsibility to our vast audience of children around the world."

"Reporters are always analyzing our approach to entertainment, but there's no magic formula. I just make what I like—warm and human stories, and ones about historic characters and events, and about animals. If there is a secret, I guess it's that I never make the pictures too childish, but always try to get in a little satire of adult foibles. Also, we do everything our own way, for ourselves, with no outside interference. We stay close to the fundamentals of family entertainment and recreation, and have complete voice in the marketing."

"I was doing this *Sorcerer's Apprentice* with Mickey Mouse and I happened to have dinner one night with [Leopold] Stokowski. And Stokowski said, 'Oh, I'd love to conduct that for you.' Well, that led to not only doing this one little short subject but it got us involved to where I did all of *Fantasia* and before I knew it I ended up spending four hundred and some odd thousand dollars getting music with Stokowski. But we were in then and it was the point of no return. We went ahead and made it."

"*Fantasia*, to me, is a whole new opportunity. For my medium it opens up unlimited possibilities. Music has always played a very important part since sound came into the cartoon. Now, the full expression that comes from the new Fantasound opens up a whole new world for us."

"In this volatile business of ours, we can ill afford to rest on our laurels, even to pause in retrospect. Times and conditions change so rapidly that we must keep our aim constantly focused on the future."

"We allow no geniuses around our studio."

"After a long concentration on live-action and cartoon films, we decided to try something that would employ about every trick we had learned in the making of films. We would combine cartoon and live action in an enormous fantasy—*Mary Poppins*. And what a far cry that was from *Snow White*. As the original *Mary Poppins* budget of five million dollars continued to grow, I never saw a sad face around the entire studio. And this made me nervous. I knew the picture would have to gross ten million dollars for us to break even. But still there was no negative head-shaking. No prophets of doom. Even Roy was happy. He didn't even ask me to show the finished picture to a banker. The horrible thought struck me—suppose the staff had finally conceded that I knew what I was doing."

"Caution there must be, of course, along with venturesome courage.

The motion picture business has long been a chance-taking business. This doesn't mean timidity in planning an operation."

"I have every confidence that so long as our film presentations toughen the mind and warm the heart with the **best** the motion picture industry can offer in art and craftsmanship and genuine human warmth, so long may we expect prosperous support and a long life."

"The motion picture will never fully replace the printed word, but it will go a long way in becoming its most valuable adjunct. There seems little question that the human mind will absorb picturized information much quicker than by means of the printed word."

"I think one reason why people like our films is that so much effort is made to give them adult as well as child appeal. Children laugh at entirely different things from those which amuse grown people. Where the subject matter is a little deep for children, amusing action must be injected to hold their interest."

"I am not influenced by the techniques or fashions of any other motion-picture company."

"In the inspiration of mind and spirit that go into the making of Disney picture-making, one essential is clarity.

The other is interest; if he is shown that it relates directly to his needs; if he is made eager to learn and learning becomes—as it can be—one of the keenest of pleasures, then he will learn far more readily and surely than if he is forced to drudge along under the whip of compulsion or duty. Failure to make clear the nature and meaning of the thing being produced is one of the surest causes of dullness and failure to learn. The success of our movies has sprung from their universal appeal to millions of people of all nations, all ages, all degrees of experience, intelligence, and learning."

"The motion picture still has great things ahead. Equipped with its big screens, its color and sound fidelities and all its perfected devices for illusionment, nothing is beyond its range and powers. Itself a marvel of science, it can and will serve with equal facility the space enthusiast looking beyond the sun, and the homebody content with the warm familiar earth and all its bounties when he goes with his family seeking entertainment and inspiration."

"The motion picture has become one of the marvels of all time; a true Wonder of the World in its magical powers. But what it has brought on the screen for every man and his family to see and ponder has been even more wonderful."

"The screen has too long been confined to what we can see and hear, what the camera can show ...

things which reveal not the half of a man's life and his most intense interests, with live actors attempting to interpret the unseen—the emotions, the impulses of the mind. And doing it, we must admit, rather clumsily most of the time. Relying largely on words often almost meaningless. Now, with the animated cartoon, we have another perfected tool—another scope—for getting at the inner nature of things and projecting them for the eye and the ear."

"If I can't find a theme, I can't make a film anyone else will feel. I can't laugh at intellectual humor. I'm just corny enough to like to have a story hit me over the heart."

"I've never believed in doing sequels. I didn't want to waste the time I have doing a sequel; I'd rather be using that time doing something new and different. It goes back to when they wanted me to do more pigs."

"The truth of the matter is that by the time we had the studio built, the banks owed me money, thanks to *Snow White*.
And it gave me more personal satisfaction than anything I have ever done because it proved to a lot of sneering critics that a full-length cartoon could make money."

"As a kid, I had seen the story and liked it. The figures of the dwarfs intrigued me. I thought it was a good plot, and it had a broad appeal. It wasn't too fantastic. That's what you need: a fairly down-to-earth story that people can associate themselves with."
(on *Snow White*)

"The success of the *Silly Symphonies* gave us the courage for *Snow White*.
And you should have heard the howls of warning! It was prophesied that nobody would sit through a cartoon an hour and a half long. But, we had decided there was only one way we could successfully do it and that was to go for broke—shoot the works. There could be no compromise on money, talent, or time. We did not know whether the public would go for a cartoon feature—but we were darned sure that audiences would not buy a bad cartoon feature."

"Animated picture-making is an expensive business. One wrong pencil line can cost hundreds of dollars. I can't hold a pencil to the artists in my studio. I credit the success of my films to the teamwork in my organization."

"In all my years of picture-making I have never had more satisfaction or felt more useful in the business of entertainment than I have in making the True-Life Adventure features."

"Women are the best judges of anything we turn out. Their taste is very important. They are the theatergoers, they are the ones who drag the men in. If the women like it, to heck with the men."

on mickey mouse

"Mickey Mouse is, to me, a symbol of independence. He was a means to an end. He popped out of my mind onto a drawing pad twenty years ago on a train ride from Manhattan to Hollywood at a time when business fortunes of my brother Roy and myself were at lowest ebb and disaster seemed right around the corner. Born of necessity, the little fellow literally freed us of immediate worry. He provided the means for expanding our organization to its present dimensions and for extending the medium of cartoon animation toward new entertainment levels. He spelled production liberation for us."

"All we ever intended for him or expected of him was that he should continue to make people everywhere chuckle with him and at him. We didn't burden him with any social symbolism, we made him no mouthpiece for frustrations or harsh satire. Mickey was simply a little personality assigned to the purposes of laughter."

"The life and ventures of Mickey Mouse have been closely bound up with my own personal and professional life.
It is understandable that I should have sentimental attachment for the little personage who played so big a part in the course of Disney Productions and has been so happily accepted as an amusing friend wherever films are shown around the world. He still speaks for me and I still speak for him."

"When people laugh at Mickey Mouse it's because he's so human; and that is the secret of his popularity."

"We felt that the public, and especially the children, like animals that are cute and little. I think we are rather indebted to Charlie Chaplin for the idea. We wanted something appealing, and we thought of a tiny bit of a mouse that would have something of the wistfulness of Chaplin—a little fellow trying to do the best he could."

"I only hope that we never lose sight of one thing—that it was all started by a mouse."

on the parks

"When we opened Disneyland, a lot of people got the impression that it was a get-rich-quick thing, but they didn't realize that behind Disneyland was this great organization that I built here at the Studio, and they all got into it and we were doing it because we loved to do it."

"Disneyland is a thing that I can keep molding and shaping. It's a three-dimensional thing to play with. But when I say, 'play with it,' I don't mean that. Everything I do I keep a practical eye toward its appeal to the public."

"Disneyland would be a world of Americans, past and present, seen through the eyes of my imagination—a place of warmth and nostalgia, of illusion and color and delight."

"When I started on Disneyland, my wife used to say, 'But why do you want to build an amusement park?

They're so dirty.' I told her that was just the point—mine wouldn't be."

"Disneyland is like Alice stepping through the Looking Glass; to step through the portals of Disneyland will be like entering another world."

"Physically, Disneyland would be a small world in itself—it would encompass the essence of the things that were good and true in American life. It would reflect the faith and challenge of the future, the entertainment, the interest in intelligently presented facts, the stimulation of the imagination, the standards of health and achievement, and above all, a sense of strength, contentment, and well-being."

"A word may be said in regard to the concept and conduct of Disneyland's operational tone. Although various sections will have the fun and flavor of a carnival or amusement park, there will be none of the 'pitches,' game wheels, sharp practices, and devices designed to milk the visitor's pocketbook."

"A lot of people don't realize that we have some very serious problems here, keepin' this thing going and gettin' it started. I remember when we opened [Disneyland], if anybody recalls, we didn't have enough money to finish the landscaping and I had Bill Evans go out and put Latin tags on all the weeds."

"I had different cost estimates; one time it was three and a half million and then I kept fooling around a little more with it and it got up to seven and a half million and I kept fooling around a little more and pretty soon it was twelve and a half and I think when we opened Disneyland it was seventeen million dollars."

"The idea for [Disneyland] came about

when my daughters were very young and Saturday was always Daddy's day with the two daughters. So we'd start out and try to go someplace, you know, different things, and I'd take them to the merry-go-round and I took them different places and as I'd sit while they rode the merry-go-round and did all these things—sit on a bench, you know, eating peanuts—I felt that there should be something built where the parents and the children could have fun together. So that's how Disneyland started. Well, it took many years . . . it was a period of maybe fifteen years developing. I started with many ideas, threw them away, started all over again. And eventually it evolved into what you see today at Disneyland. But it all started from a daddy with two daughters wondering where he could take them where he could have a little fun with them, too."

"To all who come to this happy place: Welcome. Disneyland is your land. Here, age relives fond memories of the past . . . and here youth may savor the challenge and promise of the future. Disneyland is dedicated to the ideals, the dreams, and the hard facts that have created America . . . with the hope that it will be a source of joy and inspiration to all the world."
(On opening day at Disneyland)

"I just want to leave you with this thought, that it's just been sort of a dress rehearsal and we're just getting started. So if any of you start resting on your laurels, I mean just forget it, because . . . we are just getting started."
(On the 10th anniversary of Disneyland)

"Disneyland is like a piece of clay, if there is something I don't like, I'm not stuck with it. I can reshape and revamp."

"Whenever I go on a ride, I'm always thinking of what's wrong with the thing and how it can be improved."

"It's no secret that we were sticking just about every nickel we had on the chance that people would really be interested in something totally new and unique in the field of entertainment."
(On Disneyland)

"We did it, in the knowledge that most of the people I talked to thought it would be a financial disaster—closed and forgotten within the first year."

(On Disneyland)

"The more I go to other amusement parks in all parts of the world, the more I am convinced of the wisdom of the original concepts of Disneyland.

I mean, have a single entrance through which all the traffic would flow, then a hub off which the various areas were situated. That gives people a sense of orientation—they know where they are at all times. And it saves a lot of walking."

"The idea of Disneyland is a simple one. It will be a place for people to find happiness and knowledge. It will be a place for parents and children to share pleasant times in one another's company; a place for teachers and pupils to discover greater ways of understanding and education. Here the older generation can recapture the nostalgia of days gone by, and the younger generation can savor the challenge of the future. Here will be the wonders of nature and man for all to see and understand. Disneyland will be based upon and dedicated to the ideals, the dreams and hard facts that have created America. And it will be uniquely equipped to dramatize these dreams and facts and send them forth as a source of courage and inspiration to all the world. Disneyland will be sometimes a fair, an exhibition, a playground, a community center, a museum of living facts, and a showplace of beauty and magic. It will be filled with accomplishments, the joys and hopes of the world we live in. And it will remind us and show us how to make these wonders part of our own lives."

"Disneyland will be the essence of America as we know it, the nostalgia of the past, with exciting glimpses into the future. It will give meaning to the pleasure of the children—and pleasure to the experience of adults. It will focus a new interest upon Southern California through the mediums of television and other exploitation. It will be a place for California to be at home, to bring its guests, to demonstrate its faith in the future. And, mostly as stated at the beginning—it will be a place for the people to find happiness and knowledge."

"Disneyland is a show."

"When we were planning Disneyland, we hoped that we could build something that would command the respect of the community and after ten years, I feel that we've accomplished that—not only the community but the country as a whole."

"[Disneyland is] something that will never be finished. Something that I can keep developing, keep plussing and adding to. It's alive. It will be a live, breathing thing that will need change. A picture is a thing, once you wrap it up and turn it over to Technicolor you're through. *Snow White* is a dead issue with me. A live picture I just finished, the one I wrapped up a few weeks ago, it's gone, I can't touch it. There're things in it I don't like; I can't do anything about it. I wanted something alive, something that could grow, something I could keep plussing with ideas; the park is that. Not only can I add things, but even the trees will keep growing. The things will get more beautiful each year. And as I find out what the public likes and when a picture's finished and I put it out, I find out what the public doesn't like, I can't change it, it's finished, but I can change the park, because it's alive. That is why I wanted that park."

"I don't want the public to see the world they live in while they're in [Disneyland]. I want them to feel they're in another world."

"Disneyland is not just another amusement park. It's unique, and I want it kept that way. Besides, you don't work for a dollar—you work to create and have fun."

"Disneyland will always be building and growing and adding new things . . .

new ways of having fun, of learning things, and sharing the many exciting adventures which may be experienced here in the company of family and friends."

"There are many ways that you can use those certain basic things and give

them a new decor, a new treatment. I've been doing that with Disneyland. Some of my things I've redone as I've gone along, reshaped them."

"Disneyland will never be completed.
It will continue to grow as long as there is imagination left in the world."

"To make the dreams of Disneyland come true took the combined skills and talents of hundreds of artisans, carpenters, engineers, scientists, and craftsmen. The dreams that they built now become your heritage. It is you who will make Disneyland truly a magic kingdom and a happy place for the millions of guests who will visit us now and in the future."

"Disneyland is the star. Everything else is in the supporting role."

"Disneyland is often called a magic kingdom because it combines fantasy and history, adventure and learning, together with every variety of recreation and fun designed to appeal to everyone."

"Here you leave today—and visit the worlds of yesterday, tomorrow, and fantasy."

"Well, it took many years. I started with many ideas, threw them away, started all over again. And eventually it evolved into what you see today at Disneyland."

"Here is adventure. Here is romance. Here is mystery. Tropical rivers—silently flowing into the unknown. The unbelievable splendor of exotic flowers . . . the eerie sound of the jungle . . . with eyes that are always watching. This is Adventureland."
(On Adventureland at Disneyland)

"Here is the world of imagination, hopes, and dreams. In this timeless land of enchantment, the age of chivalry, magic and make-believe are reborn—and fairy tales come true. Fantasyland is dedicated to the young-in-heart, to those who believe that when you wish upon a star, your dreams come true."
(On Fantasyland at Disneyland)

"Here we experience the story of our country's past . . . the colorful drama of Frontier America in the exciting days of the covered wagon and the stagecoach . . . the advent of the railroad . . . and the romantic riverboat. Frontierland is a tribute to the faith, courage, and ingenuity of the pioneers who blazed the trails across America."
(On Frontierland at Disneyland)

"Main Street, U.S.A. is America at the turn of the century—the crossroads of an era. The gas lamps and the electric lamp—the horse-drawn car and auto car. Main Street is everyone's hometown—the heart line of America."
(On Disneyland's Main Street, U.S.A.)

"Well, you know this Disneyland concept kept growing and growing

and finally ended up where I felt like I needed two or three hundred acres. So I wanted it in the Southern California area; had certain things that I felt I needed, such as flat land because I wanted to make my own hills. So I had a survey group go out and hunt for areas that might be useful and they finally came back with several different areas and we settled on Anaheim. The price was right but there was more to it than that, and that is that Anaheim was a sort of a growing area and the freeway project was such that we could see that eventually the freeways would hit Anaheim as a sort of a hub, so that's how we selected Anaheim."

"Anaheim was a town of 14,000 then,

and if someone had mentioned that one year soon six million visitors would come to Disneyland, folks might have had second thoughts about inviting us. In fact, we might have had second thoughts about building a Disneyland!"

"I first saw the site for Disneyland back in 1953. In those days it was all flat land—no rivers, no mountains, no castles or rocket ships—just orange groves, and a few acres of walnut trees."

"A vista into a world of wondrous ideas, signifying man's achievements . . . a step into the future, with predictions of constructive things to come. Tomorrow offers new frontiers in science, adventure, and ideals: the Atomic Age . . . the challenge of outer space . . . and the hope for a peaceful and unified world." (On Tomorrowland at Disneyland)

"Now, when we opened Disneyland, outer space was Buck Rogers. I did put in a trip to the moon. And I got Wernher von Braun to help me plan the thing. And, of course, we were going up to the moon long before Sputnik. And since then has come Sputnik and then has come our great program in outer space. So I had to tear down my Tomorrowland that I built eleven years ago and rebuild it to keep pace."

"[EPCOT is] like the city of tomorrow ought to be. A city that caters to the people as a service function. It will be a planned, controlled community, a showcase for American industry and research, schools, cultural, and educational opportunities."

"But the most exciting and by far the most important part of our Florida project . . . in fact, the heart of everything

we'll be doing in Disney World . . . will be our Experimental Prototype Community of Tomorrow! We call it EPCOT. EPCOT will be an experimental prototype community of tomorrow that will take its cue from the new ideas and new technologies that are now emerging from the creative centers of American industry. It will be a community of tomorrow that will never be completed, but will always be introducing and testing and demonstrating new materials and systems. And EPCOT will always be a showcase to the world for the ingenuity and imagination of American free enterprise. I don't believe there's a challenge anywhere in the world that's more important to people everywhere than finding solutions to the problems of our cities. But where do we begin . . . how do we start answering this great challenge? Well, we're convinced we must start with the public need. And the need is for starting from scratch on virgin land and building a special kind of new community. So that's what EPCOT is . . . an experimental prototype community that will always be in a state of becoming. It will never cease to be a living blueprint of the future, where people actually live a life they can't find anywhere else in the world. Everything in EPCOT will be dedicated to the happiness of the people who will live, work, and play here . . . and to those who come here from all around the world to visit our living showcase. We don't presume to know all the answers. In fact, we're counting on the cooperation of American industry to provide their best thinking during the planning and creation of our Experimental Prototype Community of Tomorrow. And most important of all, when EPCOT has become a reality and we find the need for technologies that don't even exist today, it's our hope that EPCOT will stimulate American industry to develop new solutions that will meet the needs of people expressed right here in this experimental community."

"We have done a lot of thinking on a model community, and I would like to be a part of building one, a city of tomorrow, as you might say. I don't believe in going out to this extreme blue sky stuff that some of the architects do. I believe people still want to live like human beings. But there are a lot of things that could be done. I'm not against the automobile but I just feel that you can design so that the automobile is there but still put people back as pedestrians again. I'd love to work on a project like that."

"But if we can bring together the technical know-how of American industry and the creative imagination of the Disney Organization—I'm confident we can create right here in Disney World a showcase to the world of the American free enterprise system."

"The one thing I learned from Disneyland was to control the environment. Without that we get blamed for the things that someone else does. When they come here they're coming because of an integrity that we've established over the years, and they drive for hundreds of miles and the little hotels on the fringe would jump their rates three times. I've seen it happen and I just can't take it because, I mean, it reflects on us. I just feel a responsibility to the public when I go into this thing that we must control that, and when they come into this so-called world, that we will take the blame for what goes on."

"Here in Florida, we have something special we never enjoyed at Disneyland . . . the blessing of size. There's enough land here to hold all the ideas and plans we can possibly imagine."

"I've always said there will never be another Disneyland, and I think it's going to work out that way. But it will not be the equivalent of Disneyland. We know the basic things that have family appeal. There are many ways that you can use those certain basic things and give them a new decor, a new treatment. This concept here will have to be something that is unique, so there is a distinction between Disneyland in California and whatever Disney does in Florida."

"Believe me, it's the most exciting and challenging assignment we have ever tackled at Walt Disney Productions."
(On Walt Disney World)

on business and the walt disney company

"The secret of juggling many responsibilities is organization.
Key men are responsible to me and constantly in touch with me to see that I'm there at the right time. These administrators keep things running."

"My big brother Roy was already in Los Angeles as a patient in the Veterans Hospital. When he got out, we had more in common than brotherly love. Both of us were unemployed . . . and neither could get a job. We solved the problem by going into business for ourselves. We established the first animated cartoon studio in Hollywood."

"Every man is captain of his career and there must be cooperation all around if he is to get what he wants out of life. There is no better time to begin learning this lesson than when we are young, and I think there is no better means of teaching it than through sports programs as well organized and supervised as Little League baseball. Baseball is a great teacher of an important secret of living: the giving and taking in the group, the development of qualities and behavior that will stand us in good stead through life in pursuits both personal and professional."

"I haven't drawn a single character in over thirty years. It's not only that I have no time for it any longer, but I've found development of the stories themselves much more intriguing than drawing. This seems all the more amazing when one considers that each film, no matter how many people have worked on it, has what is called the 'Disney Touch.' The secret is teamwork. Each character is arrived at by group effort. An artist might have a lot of talent and come up with an excellent idea, but if, after it is thoroughly analyzed, the character cannot be adapted and worked with by the group, we discard it."

"Recently someone pointed out that in the past ten years we have produced fifty-two feature-length motion pictures, exactly twice the twenty-six features we made in our first three decades, since the day in 1923 when Roy and I went into business making cartoons. Those who have followed our progress know that this figure is typical of what our imaginative staffs have accomplished in recent years, in all areas of our company. The success of *Mary Poppins* and our other films, the worldwide attraction of Disneyland Park, the impact of our color program on network television, and the popularity of our four shows at the New York World's Fair—these things give us confidence that what we do continues to have strong appeal and acceptance by the public."

"When we consider a new project, we really study it—not just the surface idea, but everything about it. And when we go into that new project, we believe in it all the way. We have confidence in our ability to do it right. And we work hard to do the best possible job."

"I wanted to retain my individuality. I was afraid of being hampered by studio policies. I knew if someone else got control, I would be restrained."

"There's really no secret about our approach. We keep moving forward—opening up new doors and doing new things—because we're curious. And curiosity keeps leading us down new paths. We're always exploring and experimenting. We call it Imagineering—the blending of creative imagination with technical know-how."

"Everyone needs deadlines. Even the beavers. They loaf around all summer, but when they are faced with the winter deadline, they work like fury. If we didn't have deadlines, we'd stagnate."

"To try to keep an operation like Disneyland going you have to pour it in there. It's what I call 'Keeping the show on the road.' Not just new attractions, but keeping it staffed properly . . . you know, never letting your personnel get sloppy . . . never let them be unfriendly. That's been our policy all our lives. My brother and I have done that and that is what has built our organization."

"The first year [at Disneyland] I leased out the parking concession, brought in the usual security guards—things like that—but soon realized my mistake. I couldn't have outside help and still get over my idea of hospitality. So now we recruit and train every one of our employees. I tell the security police, for instance, that they are never to consider themselves cops. They are there to help people. The visitors are our guests. It's like running a fine restaurant. Once you get the policy going, it grows."

"Well, I think by this time my staff, my young group of executives, and everything else, are convinced that Walt is right. That quality will out. And so I think they're going to stay with that policy because it's proved that it's a good business policy. Give the people everything you can give them. Keep the place as clean as you can keep it. Keep it friendly, you know. Make it a real fun place to be. I think they're convinced and I think they'll hang on after . . . as you say . . . well . . . after Disney."

"The way I see it, Disneyland will never be finished. It's something we can keep developing and adding to. A motion picture is different. Once it's wrapped up and sent out for processing, we're through with it. If there are things that could be improved, we can't do anything about them anymore. I've always wanted to work on something alive, something that keeps growing. We've got that in Disneyland."

"We developed so many talents as we went along that I lay awake nights figuring out how to use them. That's how we became so diversified. It was a natural branching out."

"Get in. Not choose but get in. Be part of it and then move up. I've always had that feeling about things. And it upsets me so much when people want to get into something but they're too darn choosy about what they want to do. Get in while you have a chance to at least look and see, and out of it might come something."

"A man should never neglect his family for business."

"When they come here they're coming because of an integrity that we've established over the years. And they drive hundreds of miles. I feel a responsibility to the public."

"If I were a fatalist, or a mystic, which I decidedly am not, it might be appropriate to say I believe in my lucky star. But I reject 'luck'—I feel every person creates his own 'determinism' by discovering his best aptitudes and following them undeviatingly."

"As well as I can I'm untying the apron strings—until they scream for help."

"The inevitable course of motion-picture production has now brought us to the point where we must please more people the world over than ever before, commercially and artistically. We understand this in our responsibilities to the trade as well as for our own welfare in the industry. Diversity of entertainment therefore has become our guide and watchword."

"The whole thing here is the organization.

Whatever we accomplish belongs to our entire group, a tribute to our combined effort. Look at Disneyland. That was started because we had the talents to start it, the talents of the organization. And our World's Fair shows—what we did was possible only because we already had the staff that had worked together for years, blending creative ideas with technical know-how."

"I think if there's any part I've played ...

the vital part is coordinating these talents, and encouraging these talents, and carrying them down a certain line. It's like pulling together a big orchestra. They're all individually very talented. I have an organization of people who are really specialists. You can't match them anywhere in the world for what they can do. But they all need to be pulled together, and that's my job."

"I feel there is no door which, with the kind of talent we have in our organization, could not be opened, and we hope we can continue to unlock these barriers as long as we are in the business of bringing a happy note to those who patronize our pictures."

"I'm not the perfectionist anymore. It's my staff—they're the ones always insisting on doing something better and better. I'm the fellow trying to hurry them to finish before they spoil the job. You can overwork drawing or writing and lose the spontaneity."

"You can dream, create, design, and build the most wonderful place in the world . . . but it requires people to make the dream a reality."

"No matter what the provocation, I never fire a man who is honestly trying to deliver a job. Few workers who become established at the Disney Studio ever leave voluntarily or otherwise, and many have been on the payroll all their working lives."

"Of all the things I've done, the most vital is coordinating those who work with me and aiming their efforts at a certain goal."

"Everything here at Disneyland and the studio is a team effort."

on business and the walt disney company

"We train them to be aware that
they're there mainly to help the
guest."

"Anything that has a Disney name to it
is something we feel responsible for."

"My role? Well, you know I was stumped one day when a little boy asked, 'Do you draw Mickey Mouse?' I had to admit I do not draw anymore. 'Then you think up all the jokes and ideas?' 'No,' I said, 'I don't do that.' Finally, he looked at me and said, 'Mr. Disney, just what do you do?' 'Well,' I said, 'sometimes I think of myself as a little bee. I go from one area of the studio to another and gather pollen and sort of stimulate everybody. I guess that's the job I do.'"

"I don't pose as an authority on anything at all, I follow the opinions of the ordinary people I meet, and I take pride in the close-knit teamwork with my organization."

"Whatever we accomplish is due to the combined effort. The organization must be with you or you don't get it done. . . . In my organization there is respect for every individual, and we all have a keen respect for the public."

"Most of my life I have done what I wanted to do. I have had fun on the job. I have never been able to confine that fun to office hours."

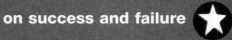 **on success and failure**

"There's a great feeling of satisfaction in winning an award for a job well done, whether it be for winning a footrace, designing a rocket, or making a motion picture. Now, we haven't done too well with the first two on the list, but pictures, that's something else. No one person can take credit for the success of a motion picture. It's strictly a team effort. From the time the story is written to the time the final release print comes off the printer, hundreds of people are involved—each one doing a job— each job contributing to the final product. And, if the picture wins an award, the feeling of satisfaction we were speaking of can rightfully be shared by each and every one."

"I have been up against tough competition all my life. I wouldn't know how to get along without it."

"Almost everyone warned us that Disneyland would be a Hollywood spectacular—a spectacular failure.
But they were thinking about an amusement park, and we believed in our idea—a family park where parents and children could have fun— together."

"All the adversity I've had in my life,
all my troubles and obstacles have strengthened me."

"I think it's important to have a good hard failure when you're young. I learned a lot out of that. Because it makes you kind of aware of what can happen to you. Because of it I've never had any fear in my whole life when we've been near collapse and all of that. I've never been afraid. I've never had the feeling I couldn't walk out and get a job doing something."

"It is good to have a failure while you're young because it teaches you so much. For one thing it makes you aware that such a thing can happen to anybody, and once you've lived through the worst, you're never quite as vulnerable afterward."

"You may not realize it when it happens, but a kick in the teeth may be the best thing in the world for you."

"To some people, I am kind of a Merlin who takes lots of crazy chances, but rarely makes mistakes. I've made some bad ones, but fortunately, the successes have come along fast enough to cover up the mistakes. When you go to bat as many times as I do, you're bound to get a good average. That's why I keep my projects diversified."

"Naturally we are all extremely gratified by the reception given *Snow White*, for it shows us conclusively that the public is ready for more animated features."

"I'd like to add one thought to the subject of success and the claims made for it as a deserved reward for effort and understanding. It seems to me shallow and arrogant for any man in these times to claim he is completely self-made, that he owes all his success to his own unaided efforts. While, of course, it is basic Americanism that a man's standing is in part due to his personal enterprise and capacity, it is equally true that many hands and hearts and minds generally contribute to anyone's notable achievement. We share, to a large extent, one another's fate. We help create those circumstances which favor or challenge us in meeting our objectives and realizing our dreams. There is great comfort and inspiration in this feeling of close human relationships and its bearing on our mutual fortunes—a powerful force to overcome the 'tough breaks' which are certain to come to most of us from time to time."

"Success often demands a big price. In my case it nearly ruined my health. The more successful I became, the harder I worked on new ideas, new developments, new techniques—until I reached a breaking point. Years ago I was close to a nervous breakdown. My doctor insisted I cut down to a five-day work week, learn to relax, and get myself some hobbies which would release my tensions."

"Get a good idea, and stay with it. Dog it, and work at it until it's done, and done right."

"People often ask me if I know the secret of success and if I could tell others how to make their dreams come true. My answer is, you do it by working."

"I suppose my formula might be: dream, diversify—and never miss an angle."

"Fun and wonder are the important elements, in addition to quality in production and performance, which are most responsible for the success of Disney productions. Fun in the sense of cheerful reaction—the appeal to love of laughter. Wonder in that we appeal to the constant wonder in men's minds, which is stimulated by imagination."

"We grew to our present size almost against ourselves. It was not a deliberately planned commercial venture in the sense that I sat down and said that we were going to make ourselves into a huge financial octopus. We evolved by necessity. We did not sit down and say to ourselves, 'How can we make a big pile of dough?' It just happened."

"I function better when things are going badly than when they're as smooth as whipped cream."

on money

"Cartoon features give us our biggest financial problems. They take a lot of manpower that could produce much more in other fields. Like most luxuries, however, there is solid value in the feature cartoon. While they're expensive, they are also prestige builders."

"Disneyland is a work of love. We didn't go into Disneyland just with the idea of making money."

"The idea for Disneyland lay dormant for several years. It came along when I was taking my kids around to these kiddie parks . . . I took them to zoos, I took them everywhere, and while they were on the merry-go-round riding forty times or something, I'd be sitting there trying to figure what I could do. When I built the studio I thought we ought to have a three-dimension thing that people could actually come and visit—they can't visit our studio because the rooms are small. So I had a little dream for Disneyland adjoining the studio, but I couldn't get anybody to go in with me because we were going through this depression. And whenever I'd go down and talk to my brother about it, why he'd always suddenly get busy with some figures, so, I mean, I didn't dare bring it up. But I kept working on it and I worked on it with my own money. Not the studio's money, but my own money."

"Everybody thinks that [Disneyland] is a gold mine—but we have had our problems. You've got to work it and know how to handle it. Even trying to keep that park clean is a tremendous expense. And those sharp-pencil guys tell you, 'Walt, if we cut down on maintenance, we'd save a lot of money.' But I don't believe in that—it's like any other show on the road; it must be kept clean and fresh."

"I could never convince the financiers that Disneyland was feasible, because dreams offer too little collateral."

"I am not an economist, but things are not as bad as they seem. I have a great deal of confidence in our future."

"Happiness is a state of mind. It's just according to the way you look at things. So I think happiness is contentment but it doesn't mean you have to have wealth. All individuals are different and some of us just wouldn't be satisfied with just carrying out a routine job and being happy."

$

**"Money is something I understand
only vaguely,** and think about it only when I don't have
enough to finance my current enthusiasm, whatever it may be. All I know
about money is that I have to have it to do things. I don't want to bank my
dividends, I'd rather keep my money working. I regard it as a moral
obligation to pay back borrowed money. When I make a profit, I don't
squander it or hide it away; I immediately plow it back into a fresh project.
I have little respect for money as such; I regard it merely as a medium for
financing new ideas. I neither wish nor intend to amass a personal
fortune. Money—or rather the lack of it to carry out my ideas—may
worry me, but it does not excite me. Ideas excite me."

"You reach a point where you don't work for money."

"Biggest problem? Well, I'd say it's been my biggest problem all my life. MONEY. It takes a lot of money to make these dreams come true. From the very start it was a problem. Getting the money to open Disneyland. About seventeen million, it took. And we had everything mortgaged, including my family. But we were able to get it open and in the ten or eleven years now we have been pouring more money back in. In other words, like the old farmer, you have to pour it back into the ground if you want it to grow. That's my brother's philosophy and mine, too."

"I've always been bored with just making money. I've wanted to do things; I wanted to build things, to get something going. What money meant to me was that I was able to get money to do that for me."

"Some people forget that you can still do good work even though you work with dollar bills. We took almost nine years to make *Fantasia*, and if we had to do it again I'd take a long hard look at it, because today it would cost us fifteen million dollars. At some stage or other I have to walk in and tell the boys, 'O.K. Start wrapping it up.' If I didn't, we'd never get the work finished. But that doesn't mean we pull back on quality."

"Recession doesn't deserve the right to exist.
There are just too many things to be done in science and engineering to be bogged down by temporary economic dislocations."

"I actually started to plan [*Snow White*] about 1935.
And I fooled around with it trying to get a hold of a story and things for a couple of years and finally it began to jell . . . then I went to work on it and I finished in the fall of 1937. I didn't know what I had or what would happen or anything. We had the family fortune . . . we had everything wrapped up in *Snow White*. In fact the bankers, I think, were losing more sleep than I was. And fortunately, though, when we put it in and premiered it and everything else, why everything was fine and the bankers were happy."

"When *Snow White* hit, we realized we were in a new business. We knew it within a week after the picture had opened at the Carthay Circle in Los Angeles. We had been heavily in debt and within six months we had millions in the bank."

on children, young and old

"Adults are interested if you don't play
down to the little two- or three-year-olds or talk down. I don't believe in
talking down to children. . . . I like to kind of just talk in a general way to
the audience. Children are always reaching."

**"You can't live on things made for
children—or for critics.** I've never made films for
either of them. Disneyland is not just for children. I don't play down."

"Despite all the publicity about delinquency, America's youngsters are a pretty good lot. One of the things I want to do is make a picture that shows the good side of teenagers. I get so put out with all these pictures about delinquency. One picture upset me for three days afterward. I think these pictures are a mistake. Children get bad ideas when they see such things on the screen. And I don't think they show a true picture of young people today."

"I do not make films primarily for children. I make them for the child in all of us, whether we be six or sixty. Call the child innocence. The worst of us is not without innocence, although buried deeply it might be. In my work I try to reach and speak to that innocence, showing it the fun and joy of living; showing it that laughter is healthy; showing it that the human species, although happily ridiculous at times, is still reaching for the stars."

"A child is helpless in choosing what is to be engraved on his mind during the formative years. The awesome responsibility is assumed, for better or worse, by us adults. Today we are shapers of the world of tomorrow. That is the plain truth. There is no way we can duck the responsibility; and there is no reason, except sloth and cowardice, why we should."

"Why do we have to grow up? I know more adults who have the children's approach to life. They're people who don't give a hang what the Joneses do. You see them at Disneyland every time you go there. They are not afraid to be delighted with simple pleasures, and they have a degree of contentment with what life has brought— sometimes it isn't much, either."

"I think of a newborn baby's mind as a blank book. During the first years of his life much will be written on the pages. The quality of the writing, whatever it be, will affect his life profoundly. Let us multiply that single mind by millions. What is written on that enormity of youthful minds will alter the course of the world. This is how history is determined. It is self-evident to anybody who studies the history of the human race."

"I didn't treat my youngsters like frail flowers, and I think no parent should. Children are people, and they should have to reach to learn about things, to understand things, just as adults have to reach if they want to grow in mental stature. Life is composed of lights and shadows, and we would be untruthful, insincere, and saccharine if we tried to pretend there were no shadows. Most things are good, and they are the strongest things, but there are evil things, too, and you could do a child no favor by trying to shield it from reality. The important thing is to teach a child that good can always triumph over evil, and that is what our pictures do."

"I regard [children] as important members of the family, and we have always considered their age, experience, and taste in selecting our theatrical productions."

"The American child is a highly intelligent human being— characteristically sensitive, humorous, open-minded, eager to learn, and has a strong sense of excitement, energy, and healthy curiosity about the world in which he lives. Lucky indeed is the grown-up who manages to carry these same characteristics over into his adult life. It usually makes for a happy and successful individual."

"While the rights and privileges of youth today are far greater than ever before, in entertainment as in other sides of their home and public life, it is still the parents who, in the main, decide what their growing youngsters may see on the screen. So it is the parents and other adult guardians of children's welfare we must satisfy."

"Movies can and do have tremendous influence in shaping young lives in the realm of entertainment toward the ideals and objectives of normal adulthood."

"My business is making people, especially children, happy. I have dedicated much of my time to a study of the problems of children."

"Children are more intelligent today because their experience is greater.

Exposure and schools are better. They have access to visual education in the schools. The imagination of the teacher is supplemented by the best visual aids. She, in turn, is stimulated and gets as much out of the films as the student does."

(On educational films)

"Every child is born blessed with a vivid imagination. But just as a muscle grows flabby with disuse, so the bright imagination of a child pales in later years if he ceases to exercise it."

"When youngsters get into serious trouble, it is generally the parents who are delinquent, not the children. If you will look a little deeper, when some unpleasant incident occurs, you'll find that there's usually something wrong in the domestic ménage. In too many cases the parents are the ones who are in trouble, and the parents are the ones who need help."

"The way to keep children out of trouble is to keep them interested in things. Lecturing to children is no answer to delinquency. Preaching won't keep kids out of trouble. But keeping their minds occupied will."

"That's the real trouble with the world, too many people grow up. They forget. They don't remember what it's like to be twelve years old. They patronize; they treat children as inferiors. I won't do that. I'll temper a story, yes. But I won't play down, and I won't patronize."

"You're dead if you aim only for kids. Adults are only kids grown up, anyway."

"Essentially, the real difference between a child and an adult is experience. We conceive it to be our job on the *Mickey Mouse Club* show to provide some of that experience. Happy, factual, constructive experience whenever possible."

"In the wintertime you can go out there during the week and you won't see any children [at Disneyland]. You'll see the oldsters out there riding all these rides and having fun and everything. Summertime, of course, the average would drop down. But the overall, year-round average, it's four adults to one child."

"[Disneyland] has that thing—the imagination, and the feeling of happy excitement—I knew when I was a kid."

"I think what I want Disneyland to be most of all is a happy place—a place where adults and children can experience together some of the wonders of life, of adventure, and feel better because of it."

"I think we have made the fairy tale fashionable again. That is, our own blend of theatrical mythology. The fairy tale of film—created with the magic of animation—is the mode equivalent of the great parables of the Middle Ages. Creation is the word. Not adaptation. Not version. We can translate the ancient fairy tale into its mode equivalent without losing the lovely patina and the savor of its once-upon-a-time quality. I think our films have brought new adult respect for the fairy tale. We have proved that the age-old kind of entertainment based on the classic fairy tale recognizes no young, no old."

"Part of the Disney success is our ability to create a believable world of dreams that appeals to all age groups. The kind of entertainment we create is meant to appeal to every member of the family."

"People sort of live in the dark about things. A lot of young people think the future is closed to them, that everything has been done. This is not so. There are still plenty of avenues to be explored."

"To the youngsters of today, I say believe in the future, the world is getting better; there still is plenty of opportunity. Why, would you believe it, when I was a kid I thought it was already too late for me to make good at anything."

"But now, looking back, I have satisfaction, even pleasure, in tracing the effects those newspaper-delivery days had on my mature life. Now I can appreciate the self-reliance, self-discipline, and self wisdom gained from those responsibilities. The sense of responsibility—yes, this I believe is the most valuable thing a boy can carry along into later life from his first job."

"It's a mistake not to give people a chance to learn to depend on themselves while they are young."

"Childishness? I think it's the equivalent of never losing your sense of humor. I mean, there's a certain something that you retain. It's the equivalent of not getting so stuffy that you can't laugh at others."

"It's a thing I remembered as a kid.

I saw Marguerite Clark in [*Snow White*] in Kansas City one time when I was a newsboy. . . . It was probably one of my first big feature pictures I'd ever seen. . . . But anyways, to me, I thought it was a perfect story. I had the sympathetic dwarfs, you see? I had the heavy; I had the prince and the girl, the romance. I just thought it was a perfect story."

on family

"The important thing is the family.
If you can keep the family together—and that's the backbone of our whole business, catering to families—that's what we hope to do."

"The most important thing brought about in the past quarter century of motion-picture history is the recognition that amusement, recreation, mass diversion, is no longer a dispensable luxury. Family fun is as necessary to modern living as a kitchen refrigerator."

"People are always analyzing our approach to entertainment. Some reporters have called it the 'special secret' of Disney entertainment. Well, we like a little mystery in our films, but there's really no secret about our approach. We're interested in doing things that are fun—in bringing pleasure and especially laughter to people. And we have never lost our faith in family entertainment—stories that make people laugh, stories about warm and human things, stories about historic characters and events, and stories about animals."

"We think of the family audience. Mickey Mouse would not have been the success he was were it not for the broad appeal. We are not playing just for kids. If you took your kids to the movies and left them there to be picked up later and did not go in yourself, I'd feel unhappy. After all, if you are aiming at the kids, what age would you aim at?"

"We're all proud of the honors that many groups around the world have given us. And we're even more proud that the public—whether in theaters, at Disneyland, or in their homes—continues to express its faith in the kind of family entertainment we produce."

"We try it in everything we do here, you know . . . for the family. We don't actually make films for children. But we make films that children can enjoy along with their parents."

"A family picture is one the kids can take their parents to see and not be embarrassed. I think that by producing family films we reach the audience which has been dormant at the box office for a long time. I don't like downbeat pictures and I cannot believe that the average family does either. Personally, when I go to the theater I don't want to come out depressed. That's why we make the kind of films so many label 'family type.' We avoid messages and have opened up new doors and broadened the field for ourselves by producing human stories, with comedy and drama mixed."

on education

"You'll be a poorer person all your life if you don't know some of the great stories and the great poems. But the actual world of nature and human nature is where you will live and work with your neighbors and your competitors. So keep your eyes open."

"There is more treasure in books than in all the pirates' loot on Treasure Island and at the bottom of the Spanish Main . . . and best of all, you can enjoy these riches every day of your life."

"It has always been my hope that our fairy-tale films will result in a desire of viewers to read again the fine, old original tales and enchanting myths on the home bookshelf or school library. Our motion picture productions are designed to augment them, not to supplant them."

"Everyone has been remarkably influenced by a book, or books. In my case it was a book on cartoon animation. I discovered it in the Kansas City Library at the time I was preparing to make motion-picture animation my life's work. The book told me all I needed to know as a beginner—all about the arts and the mechanics of making drawings that move on the theater screen. From the basic information I could go on to develop my own way of movie storytelling. Finding that book was one of the most important and useful events in my life. It happened at just the right time. The right time for reading a story or an article or a book is important. By trying too hard to read a book that, for our age and understanding, is beyond us, we may tire of it. Then, even after, we'll avoid it and deny ourselves the delights it holds."

"Crowded classrooms and half-day sessions are a tragic waste of our greatest national resource—the minds of our children."

"No one can have a well-rounded education without some knowledge of what goes on in the physical world around us. He must have some orderly information about the earth and its multitude of animal wayfarers. They have helped define our culture, our arts, our behaviorism, and, indeed, the fundamentals of our human civilization."

"The theater of education will be any marketplace, public square, hill, or dale where power can be found to project a motion picture on a screen."

"The age we're living in is the most extraordinary the world has ever seen. There are whole new concepts of things, and we now have the tools to change these concepts into realities. We're moving forward. In terms of my work, I believe people want to know about this universe that keeps unfolding before them. But let's be clear about one thing—I'm not trying to teach anything to anybody. I want to entertain the public."

"We have long held that the normal gap between what is generally regarded as 'entertainment' and what is defined 'educational' represents an old and untenable viewpoint."

"The first thing I did when I got a little money to experiment, I put all my artists back in school. The art school that existed then didn't quite have enough for what we needed, so we set up our own art school."

"Picture audiences want to know things rather than escape realities, so long as they are presented as entertainment. There now is such passion for learning as has never before swept this country and the world."

"School-age youngsters are capable of absorbing and retaining a tremendous amount of learning. Given the chance, they have an amazing aptitude for knowledge. We must not deny them that chance through shortages of classrooms and inadequate educational facilities. Having spent most of my life observing their potential, I feel convinced that a full-time education for our youth is our best investment in the future."

"I am not trying to be a teacher. I want to make stories to apply to a broad field, so that mother and father can understand the need and will help the child. If we can accomplish that, our work has been worthwhile."

"The assurance to academic leaders that 'we also teach' in the expanding scheme of public education will continue to be an inspiration to all of us who share as a team in the production of pictures which are intended to, at once, delight the senses and to appeal to the mind."

"We have always tried to be guided by the basic idea that, in the discovery of knowledge, there is great entertainment—as, conversely, in all good entertainment there is always some grain of wisdom, humanity, or enlightenment to be gained."

"Humans learned life's lessons by seeing real things or pictures with their eyes for ages before they began learning through written or spoken words, so it is not strange that they still learn most readily by pictures. The animated cartoon can set forth anything from a world in evolution to the whirl of electrons invisible to human eyes; can produce a mosquito tall enough to tower over a village or a fairy small enough to dance on a leaf; can get inside a complex machine, slow down its action, explain its operation to apprentices with a clarity impossible in any other medium, and can even get inside the human body."

"We learned a great deal during the war years when we were making instruction and technological films in which abstract and obscure things had to be made plain and quickly and exactly applicable to the men in the military services. These explorations and efficiencies of our cartoon medium must not be unused in the entertainment field."

"Educational films will never replace the teacher. The three R's are basic (reading, 'riting, 'rithmetic), but their advancement by means of the motion-picture screen will give more people in this world an opportunity to learn. Pictures can make both teaching and learning a pleasure. And educators agree that when a student has begun to learn and like it, half their problem is solved."

"The future of the animated educational movie seems as limitless as the variety of things we can portray in it."

"Recently our animation techniques have been applied to scientific subjects, accomplishing the feat of translating the abstractions of biology, chemistry, astronomy, and space engineering into popularly understood terms of theatrical entertainment."

"The cartoon is a good medium to stimulate interest. It is an ideal medium for teaching and it has always been my hope that we could do something that way. But it would have to be of general interest, yet helpful in teaching. It should be used for opening people's minds and meeting their needs. We have recently explained mathematics in a film and in that way excited public interest in this very important subject. *Donald in Mathmagic Land* stimulated interest in mathematics and turned out very well."

"I do not want to make teaching films. If I did, I would create a separate organization. It is not higher education that interests me so much as general mass education."

"The possibilities of the animated cartoon as a medium of education is virtually limitless. Its field is bound only by the capability of men to use it for its full possibilities."

"The medium of the animated film is perhaps the most flexible, versatile, and stimulating of all teaching facilities. The question now is where, how, and with what means the educational film shall be included in the tool kit of the educators."

"Equally important and absorbing, both as information and as sheer entertainment, will be our ventures

into the world of the invisible and the inaudible: Things like the processes going on in a man's body, or the functioning of his mind."

"In considering our films from a formal educational viewpoint and as an example of technical practice, the factual

nature picture presents unique possibilities. Nature herself offers as exciting documents her own living creatures. They are not obscure abstractions."

(On True-Life Adventures)

"When the subject permits, we let fly with all the satire and gags at our command. Laughter is no enemy to learning."

"I've always had the feeling and I've always felt that there's a thing that schools should put more emphasis on . . . that is, how to research. I think it is what more students should know. Take even a lawyer who's spent years in school. Where would he be without his library? I see writers who're supposed to be well-educated and everything else. You go in where they're working, you see all the different books they have around and everything else and the dictionaries they have there, the tools of their trade."

"Our heritage and ideals, our code and standards—the things we live by and teach our children—are preserved or diminished by how freely we exchange ideas and feelings."

"More than ever, I believe in the permanence of any well-founded institution which recognizes and caters to the basic needs of the people, spiritually as well as materially. And in my opinion, entertainment in its broadest sense has become a necessity rather than a luxury in the life of the American public."

"Physical America—the land itself—should be as dear to us all as our political heritage and our treasured way of life. Its preservation and the wise conservation of its renewable resources concerns every man, woman, and child whose possession it is."

"Once a man has tasted freedom he will never be content to be a slave.
That is why I believe that this frightfulness we see everywhere today is only temporary. Tomorrow will be better for as long as America keeps alive the ideals of freedom and a better life. All men will want to be free and share our way of life. There must be so much that I should have said, but haven't. What I will say now is just what most of us are probably thinking every day. I thank God and America for the right to live and raise my family under the flag of tolerance, democracy, and freedom."

"Laughter is America's most important export."

"Actually, if you could see close in my eyes, the American flag is waving in both of them and up my spine is growing this red, white, and blue stripe."

"Recently I was invited to see a show on America, and as I sat there watching and listening I felt both proud and thrilled; thrilled with the voices, thrilled with the sounds; proud of the group of one hundred talented young Americans singing about our country. The songs that made me proud of being an American."

"In my view, wholesome pleasure, sport, and recreation are as vital to this nation as productive work and should have a large share in the national budget."

"Americans are a responsive people and the ideas, the knowledge, and the emotions that come through the television screen in our living rooms will most certainly shape the course of the future for ourselves and our children."

"I get red, white, and blue at times."

on animals and nature

"Fable animals are not real animals.

They are human beings in the guise of bird and beast. From his earliest beginnings, as his cave drawings eloquently attest, man has been telling many of his experiences and dramatic conclusions and comments through animal symbols."

"I have learned from the animal world,

and what everyone will learn who studies it is, a renewed sense of kinship with the earth and all its inhabitants."

"Next to his own most intimate self-concerns, man is most fascinated by creatures of the animal kingdom. They have been close to his interest and his fate from time beyond the Ark."

"People often ask me where we find our stories about animals . . . and my answer is that Nature herself writes them. The wonders of nature are endless. . . . Sometimes we can recognize ourselves in animals—that's what makes them so interesting."

"Why do animals dominate animated cartoons? Because their reaction to any kind of stimulus is expressed physically. Often the entire body comes into play. Take a joyful dog. His tail wags, his torso wiggles, his ears flap. He may greet you by jumping on your lap or by making the circuit of the room, not missing a chair or a divan. He keeps barking, and that's a form of physical expression, too; he stretches his big mouth. But how does a human being react to a stimulus? He's lost the sense of play he once had and he inhibits physical expression. He is the victim of a civilization whose ideal is the unbotherable, poker-faced man and the attractive, unruffled woman. Even the gestures get to be calculated. They call it poise. The spontaneity of the animal—you find it in small children, but it's gradually trained out of them."

on animals and nature *183*

"Animals have personalities like people and must be studied."

"I have a great love of animals and laughter."

"All cartoon animals must be judged by their story intent and relationship as a matter of basic procedure in creating animation entertainment. Cartoon animals, of course, are not and never were replicas of real animals; they are a special breed of creatures out of the world of fable who duplicate human traits and foibles rather than those of the real animal kingdom. Mickey Mouse was never a mouse or anything like a mouse; no more than Donald was ever a duck."

"We can learn a lot from nature in action. Among other things, this: Each creature must earn his right to live and survive by his own efforts, according to his wit and energy and the things which in human relations we call moral behavior."

"Despite their countless numbers, few people ever glimpse more than the commonest breed of birds and beast. Nature—if we may speak of her as a universal intelligence—jealously guards her secret activities."

"I don't like formal gardens. I like wild nature. It's just the wilderness instinct in me, I guess."

"The immediate need for education and practice in using our natural resources of soil, forest, water, wildlife, and areas of inspirational beauty to the best advantage of all, for this generation and others to come, is again apparent to every observant citizen. My interest in these problems has been sharpened by our motion-picture production of wildlife subjects and the relation of animal life to all the other conservation issues during the past few years."

"If certain events continue, much of America's natural beauty will become nothing more than a memory. The natural beauty of America is a treasure found nowhere else in the world. Our forests, waters, grasslands and, wildlife must be wisely protected and used. I urge all citizens to join the effort to save America's natural beauty . . . it's our America—do something to preserve its beauty, strength, and natural wealth."

on animals and nature   *187*

"Sheer animated fantasy is still my first and deepest production impulse.

The fable is the best storytelling device ever conceived, and the screen is its best medium. And, of course, animal characters have always been the personnel of fable; animals through which the foibles as well as the virtues of humans can best and most hilariously be reflected."

"When I first saw Mineral King, I thought it was one of the most beautiful places in the world, and we want to keep it that way. With its development we will prove once again that man and nature can work together to the benefit of both."

"Our whole master plan for this region is based on two very important needs. First is the necessity to preserve the great natural beauty of the site. That is a must. Second, we want Mineral King to become a year-round recreational facility for everyone, regardless of age or athletic abilities." (About a proposed development in Calfornia's Sierra Nevada)

"Our wish to develop Mineral King is a logical outgrowth of our experience and interest. For more than ten years, nature and the outdoors have been dominant themes in our films, television shows, and our activities at Squaw Valley."

"To all of us, the development of Mineral King represents both a challenge and an obligation; a challenge to create, design, and operate facilities that serve the ever-growing public need and the interest of participants. It is also an obligation to preserve nature's gifts to Mineral King."

"It is our plan to make Mineral King a year-round recreational adventure for everyone . . . a challenge to the accomplished skier and a good place to put skis on for the first time . . . the ideal spot for an old-fashioned family outing . . . home base for wildlife students, hikers, fishermen, and campers . . . the perfect retreat for those who just want to get away for a breath of fresh, invigorating mountain air."

"When we go into a new project, we believe in it all the way. That's the way we feel about Mineral King. We have every faith that our plans will provide recreational opportunities for everyone. All of us promise that our efforts now and in the future will be dedicated to making Mineral King grow to meet the ever-increasing public need. I guess you might say that it won't ever be finished."

"We believe that Mineral King should be much more than the best place to spend a vacation or holiday. We want it to be an experience with the outdoors for those who love nature—or who want to learn to love it."

"We did not succumb to the alluring temptations to make villains or saints of the creatures portrayed in our [True-Life Adventure] films. We have maintained a sensitive regard for the wisdom of Nature's design and have attempted to hold a mirror to the out-of-doors rather than to interpret its functioning by man's standards. Our films have provided thrilling entertainment of educational quality and have played a major part in the worldwide increase in appreciation and understanding of nature. These films have demonstrated that facts can be as fascinating as fiction, truth as beguiling as myth, and have opened the eyes of young and old to the beauties of the outdoor world and aroused their desire to conserve priceless natural assets."

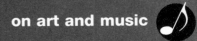
on art and music

"I don't pretend to know anything about art. I make pictures for entertainment, and then the professors tell me what they mean."

"I've never called my work an 'art.' It's part of show business, the business of building entertainment."

"I am in no sense of the word a great artist, not even a great animator; I have always had men working for me whose skills were greater than my own. I am an idea man."

"I like symphonic music. A good concert, if you're kind of relaxed, it can do something to you. It's sort of an emotional break you get by listening to the music."

"Music has always had a prominent part in all our products, from the early cartoon days. So much so, in fact, that I cannot think of the pictorial story without thinking about the complementary music which will fulfill it. Often the musical theme comes first, suggesting a way of treatment. This was the case with the Tchaikovsky music for *Sleeping Beauty* which finally formulated our presentation of the classic. I have had no formal musical training. But by long experience and by strong personal leaning, the selection of musical themes, original or adapted, we were guided to wide audience acceptance. Credit for the memorable songs and scores must, of course, go to the brilliant composers and musicians who have been associated with me through the years."

"Possibly the *Three Little Pigs* came out at just the right psychological moment—in 1933 a lot of people were talking about keeping the wolf [the Depression] from the door. At any rate, both the picture and song were quite successful—and important to us in another way as well. They showed us the value of telling a story through a song. When we started *Snow White*, the first feature-length cartoon, we kept this in mind. Of course, we wanted the songs to stand on their own merits . . . and most of them did very well. But our first concern was to make sure that each song helped us tell our story."

"Throughout our career in motion pictures, classical music has played a very important part. Early in the beginning we created a cartoon series called Silly Symphonies . . . simple short subjects that relied heavily on the works of classical composers. The popularity of the Silly Symphonies led us to undertake a major effort, *Fantasia*, which featured the music of Bach, Dukas, Tchaikovsky, Stravinsky, Mussorgsky, Beethoven, and Schubert."

"It's no more a cartoon than a painting by Whistler is a cartoon."

(On *Snow White*)

on progress and innovation

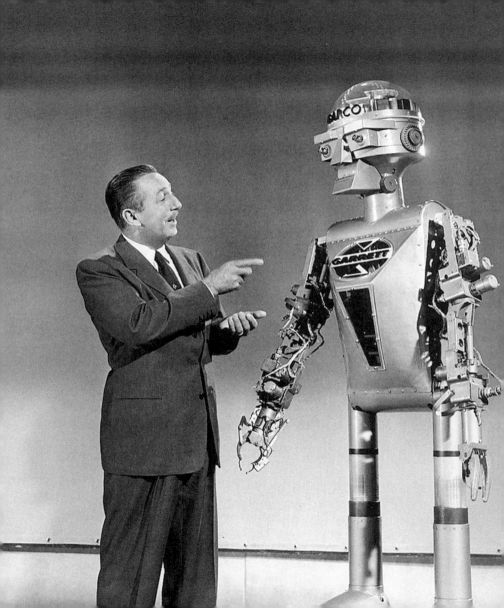

"[Audio-Animatronics® are] just another dimension in the animation we have been doing all our life."

"Our whole forty-some-odd years here has been in the world of making things move—inanimate things move.
From a drawing board through all kinds of any little props and things. Now, [with Audio-Animatronics®] we're making these human figures, dimensional human figures move, making animals move, making anything move through the use of electronics. It's a tape mechanism, it's like programming or sequencing when they're sending missiles to the moon."

on progress and innovation *205*

"I figured it would take me ten years to get Mr. Lincoln going. Well, I had him in what

we called *Mark I* and I had him under manual control. We could make him stand up and put his hand out. Robert Moses was getting the World's Fair going, and he came out. He came and visited Disneyland. He wanted to visit the studio. He was trying to get ideas on what could be done. So I had him meet Abraham Lincoln. I said, 'Would you like to meet Mr. Lincoln?' He gave me a funny look. I said, 'Well, come on in—meet him.' So when he walked in the door, I said, 'Mr. Lincoln, meet Mr. Moses,' and Lincoln stood up and put his hand out and Moses went over and shook hands with him. Well, Moses is quite a showman and he said, 'I've got to have Lincoln in the Fair.' But I said, 'This is five years away, anyway.' But Moses wouldn't take no for an answer. The next thing I knew he had gotten with the State of Illinois and was trying to sell them on a Pavilion. And before I knew it, I had my arm twisted and I said, 'Yes.' We now had to get Mr. Lincoln on the road, I think, in about thirteen months." (On the 1964 New York World's Fair exhibit Great Moments With Mr. Lincoln)

"[Audio-Animatronics® are] sound and animation through electronics. It's opened a whole new door for us. We can program whole shows on a tape. The tape sends signals and the little figures go to work and they sing and act and move according to the impulse that comes from the tape. And this is all possible because of this big drive that we've had on the space age development, the electronic age."

"Attractions will 'come to life' through Audio-Animatronics®, our space-age electronic method of making inanimate things move on cue, hour after hour and show after show."

"Of all our inventions for mass communication, pictures still speak the most universally understood language."

"It is to the nature of our communications that we must look for the benefactions which can come from such interchange. The machinery stands ready, is already widely in use, and will become perhaps incredibly more so as we put science to our humanitarian uses."

"Direct and easy communications— freedom of speech in all forms and its broadest sense—has become vital to the very survival of a civilized humanity."

"It is the source of public information and what we say to these massive receptive audiences which pose the problems and the challenges of our time."

"All of us who use the implements of mass communications have tremendous responsibility to utilize them more fully in the interest of common humanity in the light of present world conditions."

"It is a curious thing that the more the world shrinks because of electronic communications, the more limitless becomes the province of the storytelling entertainer."

"I believe in being an innovator."

"You hate to repeat yourself. I don't like to make sequels to my pictures. I like to take a new thing and develop something, a new concept."

on television

"Our contribution to television is entertainment, created without deviation from our conception of what entertainment should be."

"Again, we feel, there is a strong secondary value here—in that watching the Mouseketeers and their guests in action, boys and girls in homes throughout the land will feel impelled to discover and develop their own talents, whatever they may be."

"Many times recently we have been asked this question: What is the difference in technique between TV and motion-picture production at the Walt Disney Studios? The answer to that, except in the theatrical use of CinemaScope®, there is no appreciable difference. We go through the same motions. There are just many more of them when you produce for the two media."

"Television began to move and I began to think about it. I talked to a lot of these television executives and they said, 'What are you going to do? If you go on television what are you going to do?' I said, 'I don't know. I presume I'll do what I've been doing all my life.' They said, 'Well, television is different, you've got to do something different.' I said, 'Well, I know, but I don't think that the audience is any different.'"

"When it came to television, the one thing I wanted was to control my product. I didn't want anybody else to have it. I wanted to control the format and what I did with it. Now I have complete control, there is nobody that can tell me 'yes' or 'no.' I have it and if I fall down it's me, there's no one else to blame."

"Every time I'd get to thinking of television I would think of this park. And I knew that if I did anything like the park that I would have some kind of a medium like television to let the people know about it. So I said, 'Well here's the way I'll get my park going. It's natural for me to tie in with my television.' So it happened that I had sort of say whether we went into television or not. I had a contract that said I had complete say of what we produced. So I just sort of insisted that my Disneyland Park be a part of my television show."

"Television and the changes it has brought about in the motion-picture industry have provided an exciting new stimulus to our creative efforts. We are now able to work closer to the entertainment appetite of the public—much closer than when most of our production was animation and had to be planned in anticipation of the public's moods and market conditions well in the future. This change of pace has been very good for us, I believe, and our whole organization has gained in versatility and efficiency because of it."

"I have more latitude in television than I ever had before. When I have an idea for something I have to then go and try to sell it to the distributors, to the theater men, and everything else. But television, I just get my gang together and if we think it will be something interesting, I say, 'Let's do it.' And I go directly to my public."

"Through television I can reach my audience. I can talk to my audience. They are the audience that wants to see my pictures."

"There's a big, exciting period ahead of us, and I say it's television. Television is an open sesame to many things. I don't have to worry about going out and selling the theater man. I mean, I go right to the audience. I have a chance by getting there twenty-six times every year. I have a chance to have a pretty good batting average and not have to get in a rut."

"Instead of considering TV a rival, when I saw it, I said, 'I can use that; I want to be a part of it.'"

"Television is opening new avenues for me. You see, it's giving me new freedom, a freedom of producing things I feel we can do well, rather than having to hew down the lines of some title that somebody thinks is a prestige story . . . that the distribution people feel will sell, but maybe it is a bad story for us to fool with."

"Every motion-picture executive, whether in the production or exhibition of our industry, must be aware that television today should command our utmost respect as a medium for exploiting our wares. To ignore what is a very obvious fact is to discount one of the greatest promotional channels ever put at our disposal to reach potential box office patrons."

"We have always tried to bring moviegoers as close as possible to audience participation in our entertainment—to a feeling of intimate relationship with our cartoon characters. In Disneyland, people can actually take part in visible, touchable, moving, and dimensionable fantasy. They can ride on it, fly with it, measure imagination with it, and glean information from it about the past, the present and conjectional future. Thus, our world in miniature becomes not only a valid source for a television program but virtually a must in what I regard as an obligation to our steadfast audience within reach of the telecast."

"The growth of television as a medium of mass communication among people around the earth cannot be halted, nor much longer delayed. And eventually every land will want to share in this international audiovisual exchange of ideas, of pleasurable entertainment, and closer neighborliness."

on television

on enlightenment, exploration, and experimentation

"Out of our years of experimenting and experience we learned one basic thing about bringing pleasure and knowledge to people of all ages and conditions which goes to the very roots of public communication. That is this—the power of relating facts, as well as fables, in story form."

"As I see it, a person's culture represents his appraisal of the things that make up his life. And a fellow becomes cultured, I believe, by selecting that which is fine and beautiful in life and throwing aside that which is mediocre or phony. Sort of a series of free, very personal choices, you might say. If this is true, then I think it follows that 'freedom' is the most precious word to culture. Freedom to believe what you choose and read, think, and say and be with what you choose. In America, we are guaranteed these freedoms. It is the constitutional privilege of every American to become cultured or to grow up like Donald Duck. I believe that this spiritual and intellectual freedom which we Americans enjoy is our greatest cultural blessing. Therefore, it seems to me, that the first duty of culture is to defend freedom and resist all tyranny."

"I'm just very curious—got to find out what makes things tick—and I've always liked working with my hands; my father was a carpenter. I even apprenticed to my own machine shop here and learned the trade. Since my outlook and attitudes are ingrained throughout our organization, all our people have this curiosity; it keeps us moving forward, exploring, experimenting, opening new doors."

"The span of years has not much altered my fundamental ideas about mass amusement. Experience has merely perfected the style and the method and the techniques of presentation. My entertainment credo has not changed a whit. Strong combat and soft satire are in our story cores. Virtue triumphs over wickedness in our fables. Tyrannical bullies are routed or conquered by our good little people, human or animal. Basic morality is always deeply implicit in our screen legends. But they are never sappy or namby-pamby. And they never prate or preach. All are pitched toward the happy and satisfactory ending. There is no cynicism in me and there is none allowed in our work."

"I am interested in entertaining people, in bringing pleasure, particularly laughter, to others, rather than being concerned with 'expressing' myself with obscure creative impressions."

"Ever since the beginning of wisdom, man has been fashioning a brighter light and a stronger glass to help him probe deeper and deeper into the marvels of nature's secret world. Today, with the modern microscope, we can peer into dark corners we've never seen before. Often we can't explain what we see, but just looking is always a dramatic and thrilling experience."

on enlightenment, exploration, and experimentation *233*

"I can never stand still. I must explore and experiment. I am never satisfied with my work. I resent the limitations of my own imagination."

"There are fashions in reading, even in thinking. You don't have to follow them unless you want to. On the other hand, watch out! Don't stick too closely to your favorite subject. That would keep you from adventuring into other fields. It's silly to build a wall around your interests."

"Since the beginning of mankind, the fable-tellers have not only given us entertainment but a kind of wisdom, humor, and understanding that, like all true art, remains imperishable through the ages."

"You get in, we call them 'gag sessions.' We get in there and toss ideas around. And we throw them in and put all the minds together and come up with something and say a little prayer and open it and hope it will go."

"Ideas come from curiosity. When I settle one idea, my confidence takes command; nothing can shake it, and I am constant to it until it comes a reality. Then I drop it abruptly, and I rarely mention it again."

"I use the whole plant for ideas. If the janitor has a good idea, I'd use it."

"Inspiration for what we produce in television and motion pictures comes from reading, observing the world of humans around us, and also the animal kingdom."

"Courage is the main quality of leadership, in my opinion, no matter where it is exercised. Usually it implies some risk—especially in new undertakings. Courage to initiate something and to keep it going—pioneering and adventurous spirit to blaze new ways, often, in our land of opportunity."

on enlightenment, exploration, and experimentation *237*

"We have taken a new look at our world of nature and humans with the questing cameras; discarding some ancient myths and adding dimension to our scope of interests in the minds and hearts of people. The sciences, medicine, psychology, and others have taken their place alongside the arts, the romantic and fantastic in common human interest. We seek to estimate the future and its bearing on our existence, as well as dwelling fondly on the past or indulging escapist dreams."

"Movies are a medium of expression, say, like a symphony orchestra. Or like a painter's brush and canvas. The brush and canvas have been creating and presenting pictures for hundreds of years, but I haven't heard anyone say that painting was old-fashioned and had reached its limits. It's the painter—and the moviemaker—the artist and the entertainer who have to be considered—not the tools of their trade. Like painting or music, it's the ideas and the material that get onto the screen that's important. Moving pictures can be and will be new and fresh and exciting as long as there are ideas and talent in the world . . . and there's never been any sign that creative people are disappearing from the world of entertainment. What is needed in addition to the creative ability is courage—courage to try new things, to satisfy the endless curiosity of people for information about the world around them. Movies became popular because they found new forms, created new sensations, and explored new fields of popular appeal."

"By nature I'm an experimenter. To this day, I don't believe in sequels. I can't follow popular cycles. I have to move on to new things. So with the success of Mickey, I was determined to diversify."

"Well, WED is, you might call it my backyard laboratory, my workshop away from work. It served a purpose in that some of the things I was planning, like Disneyland for example . . . it's pretty hard for banking minds to go with it . . . so I had to go ahead on my own and develop it to a point where they could begin to comprehend what I had on my mind."
(On Walt Elias Disney Enterprises, which later became Walt Disney Imagineering)

on life

"I have no use for people who throw their weight around as celebrities, or for those who fawn over you just because you are famous."

"Certainly we have all had great confidence at one time in our lives, though most of us lose it as we grow older. Because of my work, I've been lucky enough to retain a shred of this useful quality but sometimes, as I look back on how tough things were, I wonder if I'd go through it again."

"When you're curious, you find lots of interesting things to do. And one thing it takes to accomplish something is courage."

"The way to get started is to quit talking and begin doing."

"What must concern us more thoughtfully is subject matter. Diversity. We must appeal to a far wider range of audience interest than ever before. We must prove to the whole new audiences, particularly our alert and curious teenager, that the movies and TV can compete for their attention with all the exciting prospects and activities of their daily life in a wonderful world of facts, of splendid dreams, of inviting experiences."

"The era we are living in today is a dream coming true."

"Somehow I can't believe there are many heights that can't be scaled by a man who knows the secret of making dreams come true. This special secret, it seems to me, can be summarized in four C's. They are Curiosity, Confidence, Courage, and Constancy, and the greatest of these is Confidence. When you believe a thing, believe it all over, implicitly and unquestioningly."

"I believe that entertainment usually fulfills some vital need and normal curiosity for every man, woman, and child who seeks it."

"Faith I have, in myself, in humanity, in the worthwhileness of the pursuits in entertainment for the masses. But wide awake, not blind, faith moves me. My operations are based on experience, thoughtful observation, and warm fellowship with my neighbors at home and around the world."

"Fantasy, if it's really convincing, can't become dated, for the simple reason that it represents a flight into a dimension that lies beyond the reach of time. In this new dimension, whatever it is, nothing corrodes or gets run down at the heel, or gets to look ridiculous like, say, the celluloid collar or the bustle. And nobody gets any older."

"Nothing is ever born afraid . . . young things—human and animal, boy or black lamb—have had no experience with fear. They rely implicitly on parents—on someone bigger and stronger than themselves, to assure safety . . . on God as they grow older and threats to security multiply."

"The only problem with anything of tomorrow is that at the pace we're going right now, tomorrow would catch up with us before we got it built."

"In order to make good in your chosen task, it's important to have someone you want to do it for. The greatest moments in life are not concerned with selfish achievements but rather with the things we do for the people we love and esteem, and whose respect we need."

"I've got a lot of [ideas]. I haven't worked them out and I haven't proved them out. I carry ideas around in my head for a long time."

"People who have worked with me say I am 'innocence in action.' They say I have the innocence and unself-consciousness of a child. Maybe I have. I still look at the world with uncontaminated wonder, and with all living things I have a terrific sympathy. It was the most natural thing in the world for me to imagine that mice and squirrels might have feelings just like mine."

"I happen to be kind of an inquisitive guy and when I see things I don't like, I start thinking, why do they have to be like this and how can I improve them?"

"Leadership implies a strong faith or belief in something. It may be a cause, an institution, a political or business operation in which a man takes active direction by virtue of his faith and self-assurance. And, of course, leadership means a group, large or small, which is willing to entrust such authority to a man—or a woman—in judgment, wisdom, personal appeal, and proven competence."

"I love the nostalgic myself. I hope we never lose some of the things of the past."

"I always like to look on the optimistic side of life, but I am realistic enough to know that life is a complex matter. With the laugh comes the tears, and in developing motion pictures or television shows, you must combine all the facts of life—drama, pathos, and humor."

"Never get bored or cynical. Yesterday is a thing of the past."

"Why be a governor or a senator when you can be king of Disneyland?"

"You don't build it for yourself. You know what the people want and you build it for them."

"Deeds, rather than words, express my concept of the part religion should play in everyday life. I have watched constantly that in our movie work the highest moral and spiritual standards are upheld, whether it deals with fable or with stories of living action."

"I ask of myself, 'Live a good Christian life.' Toward that objective I bend every effort in shaping my personal, domestic, and professional activities and growth."

"I believe firmly in the efficacy of religion, in its powerful influence on a person's whole life. It helps immeasurably to meet the storm and stress of life and keep you attuned to the Divine inspiration. Without inspiration, we would perish."

"Well, my greatest reward I think is . . . I've been able to build this wonderful organization. I've been able to enjoy good health and, the way I feel today, I feel like I can still go on being a part of this thing after forty-some-odd years of the business and also have the public appreciate and accept what I've done all these years. That is a great reward."

"The inclination of my life—the motto, you might call it—has been to do things and make things which will give pleasure to people in new and amusing ways. By doing that I please and satisfy myself. It is my wish to delight all members of the family, young and old, parent and child, in the kind of entertainment my associates and I turn out of our studio in Burbank, California. I think all artists—whether they paint, write, sing or play music, write for the theater or movies, make poetry or sculpture—all of these are first of all pleasure-givers. People who like to bring delight to other people, and hereby gain pleasure and satisfaction for themselves."

"In bad times and good, I have never lost my sense of zest for life."

"Togetherness, for me, means teamwork. In my business of motion pictures and television entertainment, many minds and skillful hands must collaborate. . . . The work seeks to comprehend the spiritual and material needs and yearnings of gregarious humanity. It makes us reflect how completely dependent we are upon one another in our social and commercial life. The more diversified our labors and interest have become in the modern world, the more surely we need to integrate our efforts to justify our individual selves and our civilization."

"I am a patient listener, but opinionated to the point of stubbornness when my mind is made up."

"We get advance reactions to our movies at previews and if the women's reaction is good, I feel fine.
If it is adverse, I begin to worry. I feel women are more honest about this than men. The men are more sentimental in one way—that is, they will sit there with tears streaming down their faces and will then come out and say, 'Mfff.' They won't admit it, because they are more cynical or shy or think it unmanly to show their sentiment. But the children, of course, are the most honest of all."

"Always, as you travel, assimilate the sounds and sights of the world."

"Why worry? If you've done the very best you can, worrying won't make it any better. I worry about many things, but not about water over the dam."

photo captions